CELEBRATING AMERICA'S SPIRIT TOGETHER

THE 54TH PRESIDENTIAL INAUGURATION

CELEBRATING AMERICA'S SPIRIT TOGETHER

THE 54TH PRESIDENTIAL INAUGURATION

Matthew Naythons
PRODUCER

David Hume Kennerly
EXECUTIVE PRODUCER

Robert McNeely
DIRECTOR OF PHOTOGRAPHY

Jain Lemos
MANAGING EDITOR

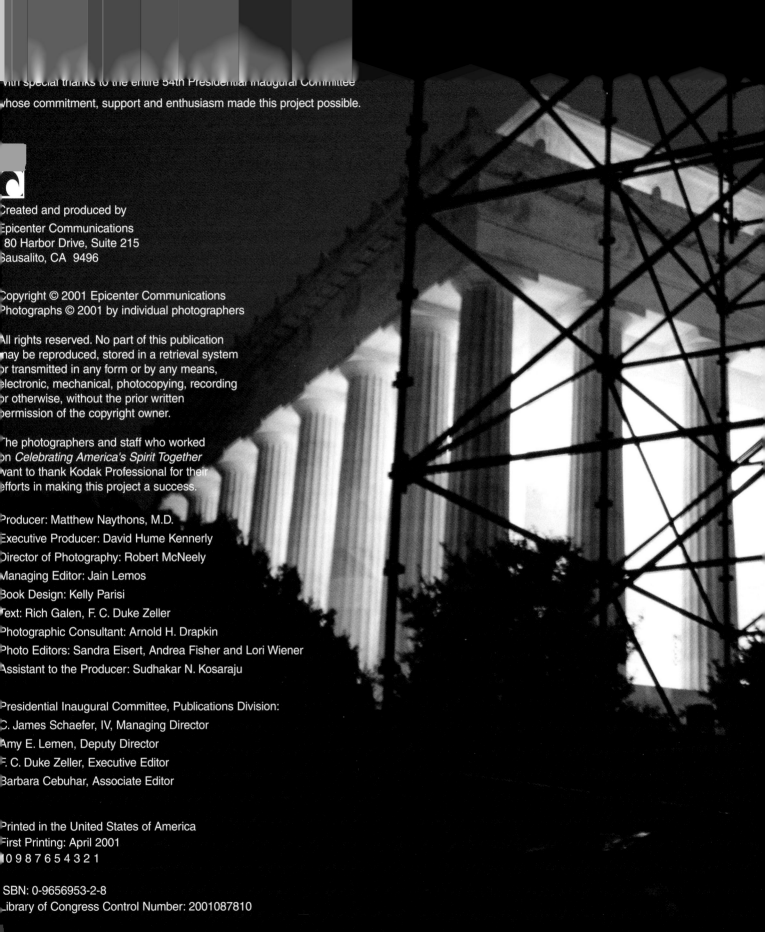

With special thanks to the entire 54th Presidential Inaugural Committee whose commitment, support and enthusiasm made this project possible.

Created and produced by
Epicenter Communications
80 Harbor Drive, Suite 215
Sausalito, CA 9496

The photographers and staff who worked
on Celebrating America's Spirit Together
want to thank Kodak Professional for their
efforts in making this project a success.

Producer: Matthew Naythons, M.D.
Executive Producer: David Hume Kennerly
Director of Photography: Robert McNeely
Managing Editor: Jain Lemos
Book Design: Kelly Parisi
Text: Rich Galen, F. C. Duke Zeller
Photographic Consultant: Arnold H. Drapkin
Photo Editors: Sandra Eisert, Andrea Fisher and Lori Wiener
Assistant to the Producer: Sudhakar N. Kosaraju

Presidential Inaugural Committee, Publications Division:
C. James Schaefer, IV, Managing Director
Amy E. Lemen, Deputy Director
F. C. Duke Zeller, Executive Editor
Barbara Cebuhar, Associate Editor

Printed in the United States of America
First Printing: April 2001
10 9 8 7 6 5 4 3 2 1

ISBN: 0-9656953-2-8
Library of Congress Control Number: 2001087810

Photograph by Hector Emanuel

The Inaugural Address:

BOUND BY IDEALS THAT MOVE US

BY PRESIDENT GEORGE W. BUSH

President Clinton, distinguished guests and my fellow citizens, the peaceful transfer of authority is rare in history, yet common in our country. With a simple oath, we affirm old traditions and make new beginnings.

As I begin, I thank President Clinton for his service to our nation. And I thank Vice President Gore for a contest conducted with spirit and ended with grace. I am honored and humbled to stand here, where so many of America's leaders have come before me, and so many will follow.

We have a place, all of us, in a long story—a story we continue, but whose end we will not see. It is the story of a new world that became a friend and liberator of the old, a story of a slave-holding society that became a servant of freedom, the story of a power that went into the world to protect but not possess, to defend but not to conquer.

It is the American story—a story of flawed and fallible people, united across the generations by grand and enduring ideals.

The grandest of these ideals is an unfolding American promise that everyone belongs, that everyone deserves a chance, that no insignificant person was ever born.

Americans are called to enact this promise in our lives and in our laws. And though our nation has sometimes halted, and sometimes delayed, we must follow no other course.

Through much of the last century, America's faith in freedom and democracy was a rock in a raging sea. Now it is a seed upon the wind, taking root in many nations.

Our democratic faith is more than the creed of our country, it is the inborn hope of our humanity, an ideal we carry but do not own, a trust we bear and pass along. And even after nearly 225 years, we have a long way yet to travel.

While many of our citizens prosper, others doubt the promise, even the justice, of our own country. The ambitions of some Americans are limited by failing schools and hidden prejudice and the circumstances of their birth. And sometimes our differences run so deep, it seems we share a continent, but not a country.

We do not accept this, and we will not allow it. Our unity, our union, is the serious work of leaders and citizens in every generation. And this is my solemn pledge: I will work to build a single nation of justice and opportunity.

I know this is in our reach because we are guided by a power larger than ourselves who creates us equal in His image.

And we are confident in principles that unite and lead us onward.

The future president makes final adjustments to his inaugural address at Blair House.
Photograph by Eric Draper

America has never been united by blood or birth or soil. We are bound by ideals that move us beyond our backgrounds, lift us above our interests and teach us what it means to be citizens. Every child must be taught these principles. Every citizen must uphold them. And every immigrant, by embracing these ideals, makes our country more, not less, American.

Today, we affirm a new commitment to live out our nation's promise through civility, courage, compassion and character.

America, at its best, matches a commitment to principle with a concern for civility. A civil society demands from each of us good will and respect, fair dealing and forgiveness.

Some seem to believe that our politics can afford to be petty because, in a time of peace, the stakes of our debates appear small.

But the stakes for America are never small. If our country does not lead the cause of freedom, it will not be led. If we do not turn the hearts of children toward knowledge and character, we will lose their gifts and undermine their idealism. If we permit our economy to drift and decline, the vulnerable will suffer most.

We must live up to the calling we share. Civility is not a tactic or a sentiment. It is the determined choice of trust over cynicism, of community over chaos. And this commitment, if we keep it, is a way to shared accomplishment.

America, at its best, is also courageous.

Our national courage has been clear in times of depression and war, when defending common dangers defined our common good. Now we must choose if the example of our fathers and mothers will inspire us or condemn us. We must show courage in a time of blessing by confronting problems instead of passing them on to future generations.

Together, we will reclaim America's schools, before ignorance and apathy claim more young lives.

We will reform Social Security and Medicare, sparing our children from struggles we have the

This jubilant monument of the seventh president of the United States, Andrew Jackson, was the first equestrian statue ever erected in the United States. *Photograph by Hector Emanuel*

power to prevent. And we will reduce taxes, to recover the momentum of our economy and reward the effort and enterprise of working Americans.

We will build our defenses beyond challenge, lest weakness invite challenge.

We will confront weapons of mass destruction, so that a new century is spared new horrors.

The enemies of liberty and our country should make no mistake: America remains engaged in the world by history and by choice, shaping a balance of power that favors freedom. We will defend our allies and our interests. We will show purpose without arrogance. We will meet aggression and bad faith with resolve and strength. And to all nations, we will speak for the values that gave our nation birth.

America, at its best, is compassionate. In the quiet of American conscience, we know that deep, persistent poverty is unworthy of our nation's promise.

And whatever our views of its cause, we can agree that children at risk are not at fault.

Abandonment and abuse are not acts of God, they are failures of love.

And the proliferation of prisons, however necessary, is no substitute for hope and order in our souls. Where there is suffering, there is duty. Americans in need are not strangers, they are citizens, not problems, but priorities. And all of us are diminished when any are hopeless.

Government has great responsibilities for public safety and public health, for civil rights and common schools. Yet compassion is the work of a nation, not just a government.

And some needs and hurts are so deep they will only respond to a mentor's touch or a pastor's prayer. Church and charity, synagogue and mosque lend our communities their humanity, and they will have an honored place in our plans and in our laws.

Many in our country do not know the pain of poverty, but we can listen to those who do.

And I can pledge our nation to a goal: When we see that wounded traveler on the road to Jericho, we will not pass to the other side.

> *"And I can pledge our nation to a goal: When we see that wounded traveler on the road to Jericho, we will not pass to the other side."*

America, at its best, is a place where personal responsibility is valued and expected.

Encouraging responsibility is not a search for scapegoats, it is a call to conscience. And though it requires sacrifice, it brings a deeper fulfillment. We find the fullness of life not only in options, but in commitments. And we find that children and community are the commitments that set us free.

Our public interest depends on private character, on civic duty and family bonds and basic fairness, on uncounted, unhonored acts of decency which give direction to our freedom.

Sometimes in life we are called to do great things. But as a saint of our times has said, every day we are called to do small things with great love. The most important tasks of a democracy are done by everyone.

I will live and lead by these principles: to advance my convictions with civility, to pursue the public interest with courage, to speak for greater justice and compassion, to call for responsibility and try to live it as well.

In all these ways, I will bring the values of our history to the care of our times.

What you do is as important as anything government does. I ask you to seek a common good beyond your comfort; to defend needed reforms against easy attacks; to serve your nation, beginning with your neighbor. I ask you to be citizens: citizens, not spectators; citizens, not subjects; responsible citizens, building communities of service and a nation of character.

Americans are generous and strong and decent, not because we believe in ourselves, but because we hold beliefs beyond ourselves. When this spirit of citizenship is missing, no government program can replace it. When this spirit is present, no wrong can stand against it.

After the Declaration of Independence was signed, Virginia statesman John Page wrote to Thomas Jefferson: "We know the race is not to the swift nor the battle to the strong. Do you not think an angel rides in the whirlwind and directs this storm?"

Much time has passed since Jefferson arrived for his inauguration. The years and changes accumulate. But the themes of this day he would know: our nation's grand story of courage and its simple dream of dignity.

We are not this story's author, who fills time and eternity with his purpose. Yet his purpose is achieved in our duty, and our duty is fulfilled in service to one another.

Never tiring, never yielding, never finishing, we renew that purpose today, to make our country more just and generous, to affirm the dignity of our lives and every life.

This work continues. This story goes on. And an angel still rides in the whirlwind and directs this storm.

God bless you all, and God bless America.

THE POWER, THE BURDEN AND THE GLORY

BY F. C. DUKE ZELLER

The office that was created with great fore-thought in 1789 by the founders of a new nation and configured by visionaries has evolved over two centuries into the most prestigious and respected post in the world. The presidency of the United States is today the greatest position of unprecedented power and incomparable responsibility on behalf of all the people of this great nation.

Every presidency begins in a spirit of rebirth and renewal—a unity that marks a coming together and a recommitment to the principles long established by our forefathers. The inauguration is an exaltation of the basic tenets of our republic to enlighten the people and elevate the nation through leadership. It is a symbol of the power and the burden that is the heritage and challenge of the American presidency.

It is a time of joy, majesty, solemnity and coming together. The inauguration of a new president is an exemplary event that serves to unify people of political differences and at once recognizes a new beginning without interruption. Every four years the people of our nation join together to witness the pageantry, to renew our faith in the republic and to participate in the peaceful transfer of power.

Facing a divided nation, Abraham Lincoln best summed up the orderly transfer of power on the eve of his inauguration in 1861: "Almost all men in this country and in any country where freedom of thought is tolerated, citizens attach themselves to political parties. It is but ordinary charity to attribute the fact that in so attaching himself to the party which his judgment prefers, the citizen believes he thereby promotes the best interests of the whole country, and when an election is passed, it is altogether befitting a free people that, until the next election, they should be as one people."

A simple oath of 35 words that has remained unchanged since first spoken by George Washington signifies the transfer of power and continuity of government. And with the deeding of authority comes renewed hope, aspirations and goals. That orderly form and coming together of differences, which is uniquely American in heritage, is worthy of celebratory recognition every four years by all citizens.

Some presidents have seen Inauguration Day as a somber and sober commencement of the most powerful job in the world, while others have reveled and gloried in the pomp and circumstance of the festivity.

After repeating the oath of office that first time in 1789, Washington, in a simple American-made brown suit of tails, is said to have kissed the Bible, adding unexpectedly, "So help me God." At the first celebration ball, he relished minueting with

Inaugural souvenirs date back as far as the first presidency and are some of the most sought-after pieces with political and presidential collectors. The Smithsonian Institution's National Museum of American History houses more than 3 million presidential objects and is by far the largest collection of its kind in the nation.

An invitation to Abraham Lincoln's second inaugural ball on March 4, 1865 (*left*) featured impressive columns with American bald eagles. Campaign buttons, such as the one for Theodore Roosevelt's run for governor (*opposite page*), are popular with collectors. Upon leaving office, Roosevelt wrote: "Although the Presidency has been very wearing ... I have thoroughly enjoyed it, for it is fine to feel one's hand guiding great machinery."

Robert Cruikshanks, fec.

President's Levee, or all Creation going to the White House

the best of New York society ladies.

On the glorious morning of his installation, James Madison commented to his wife, Dolley, "I'd much rather be in bed sleeping." That night, however, he dutifully escorted the new first lady to the inaugural ball and protectively moved her from place to place as the two ostrich feathers extending from her Parisian turban threatened to ignite or snuff out the flames of every candle in the Long Hotel ballroom.

Perhaps the most memorable inauguration of all was Andrew Jackson's in 1829. Since "Old Hickory's" beloved wife, Rachel, had died just a month before, it was decided improper to stage an inaugural ball. Instead, Jackson felt an open-house reception in the White House more appropriate and befitting his style. Crowds of thousands engulfed the mansion and overran the East Room. Food that had been carefully laid out on tables was thrown on the elegant floors and papered walls. Throughout the packed house drunken men fought, little children cried for lost parents and

An illustration of the 1829 inauguration celebration of America's seventh president, Andrew Jackson, the war hero from Tennessee. So wild was the throng of people attending the Jackson open house, that the food and beverages were ultimately moved to the lawn of the White House.

ladies fainted. There was such a press to shake Jackson's hand that he found himself trapped, almost suffocating, against the wall. A group of supporters formed a cordon around the new president and helped him escape through a side door. Mounting his horse, Jackson went back to Gadsby's Tavern and spent his first night in office there alone.

The evening before Teddy Roosevelt's inauguration, Secretary of State John Hay presented the president-elect with a gift he would cherish as long as he lived. He gave him a ring containing a lock of hair cut from Lincoln's head on the night of his assassination. The ring was handsomely engraved with the initials of both presidents and was accompanied by a handwritten note from Hay that read, "Please wear this tomorrow. You are one of the men who most thoroughly understands and appreciates Lincoln." Roosevelt later said the ring offered inspiration and encouraged him in everything he did as president.

When Dwight D. "Ike" Eisenhower became the first general in 70 years to be elected

Though his presidency only lasted a month, William Henry Harrison's inauguration in 1841 was a roaring success. The country's most popular general, "Old Tippecanoe" Harrison, brought still more supporters to the east front of the Capitol, many of whom became uneasy and unruly during the two-and-a-half-hour address.

The Gift Outright

The land was ours before we were the land's
She was our land more than a hundred years
Before we were her people. She was ours
In Massachusetts in Virginia
But we were England's, still colonials,
Possessing what we still were unpossessed by,
Possessed by what we now no more possessed.
Something we were withholding made us weak
Until we found out that it was ourselves
We were withholding from our land of living
And forthwith found salvation in surrender.
Such as we were we gave ourselves outright
(The deed of gift was many deeds of war)
To the land vaguely realizing westward,
But still unstoried artless unenhanced
Such as she was such as she would become

Robert Frost

For the Inauguration
of John F. Kennedy.

1961   To the Smithsonian

This beautifully crafted program (*far left*) was made over 100 years ago for William McKinley's inauguration in 1897 and features many symbols Americans treasure. McKinley was fond of saying, "I have never been in doubt since I was old enough to think intelligently that I would someday be made president." His swearing-in was the first to be recorded by a newfangled invention, the motion picture camera.

An 1801 hand-painted inaugural silk banner (*above*) for our nation's third president boldly proclaimed the political demise of his predecessor: "T. Jefferson, President of the United Sates of America/John Adams is no more."

At John F. Kennedy's inauguration in 1961, Robert Frost was the first poet ever to recite a poem at an inaugural ceremony. The handwritten copy of his poem "The Gift Outright" (*left*) was donated to the Smithsonian, along with a champagne bottle from one of the inaugural balls President and Mrs. Kennedy attended.

president, he also became the first to suspend the traditional formal black topper in favor of a less formal Homburg hat, more to his liking. In another first, 1952 became the first televised inauguration, although the unassuming Ike later recounted that he and Mamie were not comfortable eating their inaugural luncheon in the Old Supreme Court Chamber as millions of Americans watched live on TV.

While inaugurations are often a spectacle for millions, they can be a genuine catharsis for the American people as well. The inaugural pageantry reiterates that, although one side did not win, the new leader is going to do everything within his power to unite the nation. The inauguration is our most visible affirmation of the faith that American people have in their tenets and institutions.

It is befitting the American inaugural tradition that, at the conclusion of the festivities, George W. Bush, the 43rd president of the United States, ended the day in his new home and the home of our nation—the White House. The most historic building in the country, which is celebrating its 200th anniversary, welcomed him with a blessing engraved on one of its mantels: "I Pray Heaven To Bestow The Best of Blessings On This House And All that shall hereafter Inhabit it. May none but Honest and Wise Men ever rule under This Roof. November 1800."

F. C. Duke Zeller is an author and inaugural historian who has served five Republican presidents and three U.S. senators.

Memorabilia courtesy of the National American History Museum, Smithsonian Institution.

With the Capitol dome under reconstruction, a massive crowd gathered to witness Abraham Lincoln being sworn in for his first term as president on March 4, 1861. During his 1860 campaign, Lincoln firmly expressed his opposition to slavery and his determination to limit its expansion westward into the new territories acquired from Mexico in 1850.

At Ft. Meyer, just outside Washington, members of the U.S. Army Herald Trumpets practice for inauguration week, where they will welcome dignitaries from the public and private sectors at many events around the capital.
Photograph by Ken Cedeño

Inauguration week begins as George W. Bush leaves Texas for Washington on Wednesday, January 17, stopping first at a rally in hometown Midland, Texas. When the Bushes arrive at Andrews Air Force Base, Mr. and Mrs. Cheney lead the welcoming committee for the president-elect and future first lady. As the pace quickens, George W. Bush discusses the week's events with Campaign Chief of Staff Andrew H. Card, Jr. and Communications Director Karen P. Hughes in his office at Blair House.

Above and right: Eric Draper
Left: Karen Ballard

"I am honored to serve, and I am ready to start," the president-elect declares at the opening celebration at the Lincoln Memorial. Along the banks of the Washington Monument's Reflecting Pool, over forty thousand spectators welcome Mr. and Mrs. Bush with warm cheers on a cold evening.
Photograph by Hector Emanuel

A wonderful array of entertainers kicked off inaugural weekend. The evening was packed with performances and musical acts—military bands play, joint military forces provide an aerial salute, the Golden Knight Parachuters float to earth trailing red smoke and heavyweight boxing champion Muhammad Ali enjoys a rousing ovation. The world's most famous precision dance troupe, The Radio City Rockettes, celebrate their 75th anniversary this year.

Above: Anne Day
Right: Karen Ballard

The gifted Welsh-born 14-year-old singer Charlotte Church and the District's own mezzo-soprano Denyce Graves sparkled on stage.
Above: John Ficara
Right: Karen Ballard

The U.S. Navy Band is the Navy's premier musical representative in Washington, D.C. and is staffed by some of the nation's best musicians. As former President George Bush once noted, " ... the always impeccable, seemingly perfect, United States Navy Band."

It is a dramatic moment when the Bushes and Cheneys appear at the Lincoln Memorial statue. "It's humbling to know that I will soon take up the same office he once held," said Bush in his remarks to the audience. "I will treat the office with care, never take it for granted and always remember to whom it really belongs. It belongs to the American people."

Above: David Hume Kennerly
Right: John Ficara

Enthusiasm and continuous activity are the best recipe for keeping warm. Strangers become friends sharing this moment in history with each other.
Photograph by Hector Emmanuel

Pop music sensation Ricky Martin and President-elect Bush kid around
on stage during a performance of Martin's hit song *Cup of Life*. Sitting
with their grandmother Mrs. Jenna Welch, the Bushes' nineteen-year-old
twin daughters, Barbara Pierce Bush and Jenna Welch Bush, watch their
dad in delight. The evening is topped with the eighth consecutive—and
always dramatic—Grucci family fireworks display.
Above: David Hume Kennerly
Right: John Ficara
Fireworks: Wally McNamee

Inaugural co-chairs Kathy and Bill DeWitt and Gabrielle and Mercer Reynolds (*above*) had only five weeks to prepare for an inauguration bursting with elegant events and public festivities. For those attending—such as U.S. Senator from Mississippi Trent Lott, Indiana's Joe Watkins, who gave a moving invocation, and U.S. Senator from Texas, Kay Bailey Hutchison with her husband Ray—the pre-inaugural dinners are a chance to celebrate the beginning of a new era in American leadership.
Photographs by Anne Day

Following the opening celebration, the Bushes and Cheneys attend three elegant candlelight dinners at Union Station, the Washington Hilton and the National Building Museum. The three dinners alone host nearly 6,000 guests, yet each displays intimate touches, themed decorations and special surprises. When the Bushes and Cheneys appear, they express their deep gratitude, and Dick Cheney teases, " ... and they say those three electoral votes from Wyoming weren't important."
Photographs by David Hume Kennerly

After thanking her husband Laura Bush, herself a teacher and librarian, tells the audience at Constitution Hall, "Today is truly a librarian's dream." Mrs. Bush earned a bachelor's degree in education at Southern Methodist University and a master's degree in library science from the University of Texas at Austin. The program featured five American authors: historian Stephen Ambrose, mother-daughter mystery writers Mary Higgins Clark and Carol Higgins Clark, essayist and critic Stanley Crouch, and Texas novelist Stephen Harrigan.
Above and left: Wally McNamee

Also enjoying the event are former President George and Mrs. Barbara Bush, Mrs. Laura Bush's mother Jenna Welch and the President-elect's sister, Dorothy Koch.
Above: Anne Day
Right: Robin Bowman

Following the event celebrating America's authors, Laura Bush visited Betty Wood's fourth-grade class at William Seaton Elementary in the Shaw neighborhood of Northwest Washington with author Angela Shelf Medearis. The class was selected for the visit because it had read more books during a read-a-thon than any other class at the school. Mrs. Bush's advice to the students: "Turn off the TV and read as much as you can."

SALUTE TO AMERICA'S VETERANS

Decorated World War II veteran and former U. S. Senator Bob Dole addresses a packed house at George Washington University's Smith Center. The event, hosted by former Secretary of Defense and Vice President-elect Dick Cheney and the Armed Forces Inaugural Committee, includes a special tribute to an assembly of 101 Congressional Medal of Honor recipients.
Photograph by David Hume Kennerly

In his remarks, Vice President-elect Dick Cheney honors America's service members with these words: "Today we are saluting America's veterans by recognizing and remembering their tremendous sacrifices. The gift given to us by those who served is a recurring gift, one that we enjoy every day. We live in a free land, a land of opportunities where we can pursue our dreams. Today we salute our veterans, because we can never thank them enough." *Above: Dirck Halstead*

Connie Stevens, who for five decades has sung for troops at home and abroad, gives a gracious performance of *God Bless America*. Former Chairman of the Joint Chiefs and Secretary of State-designate Colin Powell joins former Navy pilot and U.S. Senator John McCain in honoring their fellow veterans.
Right: Dirck Halstead
Below: Karen Ballard

Col. Walter J. Marm
Service: U.S. Army
Place and date of action: Vicinity of la Drang Valley,
Republic of Vietnam, November 14, 1965.

Cpl. Rodolfo P. Hernandez
Service: U.S. Army
Place and date of action: Near Wontong-Ni, Korea,
May 31, 1951.

Chief Warrant Officer Michael J. Novosel
Service: U.S. Army
Place and date of action: Kien Tuong Province, Republic
of Vietnam, October 2, 1969.

Capt. Joseph J. Foss
Service: U.S. Marine Corps
Place and date of action: Over Guadalcanal, October 9 to
November 19, 1942, January 15 and 23, 1943.

Before a luncheon in their honor, eight of the 152 living Congressional Medal of Honor recipients pose for a portrait. The medal is our country's highest award for bravery, for the performance of acts of courage above and beyond the call of duty in battle. To find out more about all of the recipients, visit the Congressional Medal of Honor Society Web site at *www.cmohs.org*.

Capt. James M. Burt
Service: U.S. Army
Place and date of action: Near Wurselen, Germany, October 13, 1944.

Capt. Lewis L. Millett
Service: U.S. Army
Place and date of action: Vicinity of Soam-Ni, Korea, February 7, 1951.

Staff Sgt. Walter D. Ehlers
Service: U.S. Army
Place and date of action: Near Goville, France, June 9 to 10, 1944.

Spc. Charles C. Hagemeister
Service: U.S. Army
Place and date of action: Binh Dinh Province, Republic of Vietnam, March 20, 1967.

Washington D.C.'s MCI Center explodes
during the two-hour, non-stop, talent-packed
Youth Concert celebrating the energy, the
talent and the future of America's greatest
resource—our children.
Photograph by Hector Emanuel

The youth concert featured spirited performances by Jaci Velasquez, Destiny's Child, Lee Ann Womack, 98 Degrees and Jessica Simpson. A host of other notables appearing during the celebration included George P. Bush and Secretary of State-designate Colin Powell with Portia, the young woman he mentors.

Photographs by Darryl Heikes

To the surprise of the audience, President-elect Bush stops by to say hello and meet some of the children attending the celebration.
Above: John Lamb

Messages from Secretary of Housing
and Urban Development-designate
Mel Martinez and Secretary of
Education-designate Dr. Roderick R.
Paige were well received.
Above: Darryl Heikes
Right: Hector Emanuel

Former Senator Alan Simpson entertains President-elect Bush with his unique brand of humor at the Wyoming State Society reception in the Hall of Flags at the Chamber of Commerce building. Supporters, friends and family from home—plus a few surprises including the music of Hank Williams, Jr.—greeted the vice president-elect and Lynne Cheney.
Above: Dirck Halstead
Right and far right: Robin Bowman

BLACK TIE & BOOTS BALL

The Texas-sized Black Tie & Boots Ball, sponsored by the Texas State Society and held at the Marriott Wardman Park Hotel, was far and away the hottest ticket in town. Everything about the bash was big: live longhorn steers, two tons of barbecued ham and beef, 35,000 jumbo shrimp and 10,000 "Texans." *Photograph by Ken Cedeño*

Members of the Texas A&M University Ross Volunteers salute arriving guests, including hosts of the event, the bipartisan Texas State Society and the Texas Congressional Delegation. Ladies are advised, "leave your spike heels at home" to be able to navigate virtually every public space in the hotel including nine stages in seven ballrooms, a Texas Fair and Marketplace, the Lone Star Sports Bar, Hondo Honky Tonk Saloon, Cotulla Cantina and the Muleshoe Cigar and Martini Bar.
Above: Dennis Brack
Right above: Anne Day
Right bottom: Robert McNeely

Country music giants Tanya Tucker, Clint Black, Mark Chestnut, and Asleep at the Wheel, provide foot-stomping fun in the main ballroom.
Above: David Burnett
Left: Ken Cedeño

Hometown favorites the Kilgore Rangerettes and the Wildcat Wranglers dance up a storm.
"It's not every day a person we know and love becomes president of the United States," said Texas
Senator Phil Gramm. "I love you! And I love Texas!" Bush responds to the cheering audience.
Above and right above: David Burnett
Right below: Ken Cedeño

At dawn, the Capitol dome stands ready, and one of the many groups participating in the parade crosses the Memorial Bridge into the city. "Today we affirm a new commitment to live out our nation's promise through civility, courage, compassion and character," said President Bush in his inaugural address.
Above: Anne Day
Left: John Lamb

At a workshop in Lanham, Maryland, finishing touches are added to the inaugural seal that will crown the president's reviewing stand for the parade. In preparation, workers put in 12-hour days for weeks constructing floats for the parade. At Ft. Meyer, Staff Sgt. Todd Taylor of The U.S. Army Ceremonial Band, one of 10 ensembles in the U.S. Army Band, rehearses a flourish.
Left: Hector Emanuel
Below: Ken Cedeño

On the Senate side of the Capitol's west front, platoon members of the Old Guard Presidential Salute Gallery, U.S. Infantry, 3rd Division, prepare the cannons for their 21-gun salute. Spc. Jason Gray makes some final elevation adjustments.
Above: Robin Bowman

The Bushes and Cheneys begin Inauguration Day with a private prayer service at St. John's Episcopal Church, located on Lafayette Square across Pennsylvania Avenue from the White House. Immediately following, the president- and vice president-elect's families join President and Senator Clinton and Vice-President and Mrs. Gore at the White House to share a cup of coffee and good wishes before leaving for the swearing-in ceremonies at the Capitol. Inside, the Cheneys chat with Senator Mitch McConnell of Kentucky, Chairman of the Joint Congressional Committee on Inaugural Ceremonies.
Above and left: Karen Ballard
Far left: Darryl Heikes

The huge crowd spills over to the Washington Mall, where it watches George W. Bush take the oath of office on a giant screen. A father and daughter join U.S. Army Chorus member Staff Sgt. Alec Maly singing the national anthem.
Photographs by Arthur Grace
Previous pages: Robert McNeely

A rising sense of anticipation is evident on the faces of guests such as Secretary of State-designate Gen. Colin Powell. The former president and first lady are applauded as they arrive to watch their son take the oath of office. It was just 12 years ago that George Herbert Walker Bush recited the oath of office, making him the 41st president of the United States. When George W. Bush was sworn in as our 43rd president, it was only the second time in U.S. history that a son had followed his father into office. (John Quincy Adams became our sixth president in 1825 after his father, John Adams, had served from 1797 to 1801.)
Above: John Ficara

The U.S. Marine Band performs many patriotic songs for the ceremonies including *Washington's Grand March* written for President George Washington and *Alexander Reinagle's Jefferson's March* composed for President Thomas Jefferson. The band is celebrating its 200th year of presidential inaugurals and is America's oldest professional musical organization.
Above: John Ficara
Left: John Lamb

Joint Operation Center <small>PHOTOGRAPHS BY SAM KITTNER</small>

Meanwhile, back at headquarters, representatives of the FBI, the Federal Emergency Management System, the military and local police and fire jurisdictions study multiple television feeds of the inaugural events. The center, located in the building that housed the offices of the Presidential Inaugural Committee, coordinates the military's support for inaugural week events.

Members of the military and civilian safety agencies practiced for months to coordinate planned activities as well as to prepare for a wide-range of potential emergencies. Every aspect of Inauguration Day was rehearsed, from moving thousands of people from the Capitol grounds to the parade route, to opening and closing streets to traffic, to monitoring the number of passengers using Washington's Metro subway system.

Chief Justice of the Supreme Court, the Honorable William H. Rehnquist, administers the vice presidential oath of office to Richard B. Cheney as Mrs. Cheney and daughters Elizabeth and Mary look on. Among the government officials in attendance are former Presidents Jimmy Carter, George Bush and Bill Clinton, Senator Mitch McConnell, head of the Joint Committee for Inaugural Ceremonies, House Majority Leader Dick Armey, Speaker of the House Dennis Hastert, Senate Majority Leader Trent Lott and House Republican Whip Tom DeLay. Immediately following the oaths of office, the president and vice president are honored with the traditional 21-gun salute.

Above: John Ficara
Left: Robin Bowman

At noon on January 20, 2001, George W. Bush, joined by his wife and daughters, is sworn in as the nation's 43rd president with the words "I do solemnly swear that I will faithfully execute the office of President of the United States, and will to the best of my abilities preserve, protect, and defend the Constitution of the United States, so help me God."
Above: David Hume Kennerly

With an emotional hug from his dad, and a wave to the elated crowd, words from President Bush's inaugural address moments earlier still ring in the air: "Never tiring, never yielding, never finishing, we renew that purpose today, to make our country more just and generous; to affirm the dignity of our lives and every life. This work continues. This story goes on. And an angel still rides in the whirlwind and directs this storm."

Photographs by David Burnett

President Bush signs the first executive order of his new term flanked by Senator Mitch McConnell, Senate Majority Leader Trent Lott, Vice President Dick Cheney, Senate President Pro Tempore Strom Thurmond, Speaker of the House Dennis Hastert, Senior Democrat on the Joint Congressional Committee on Inaugural Ceremonies Chris Dodd and House Majority Leader Dick Armey. The new president then moved to Statuary Hall for the traditional lunch with members of Congress.

A team of 57 from Long Beach, Calif., carries the 82-by-47-foot American "super flag" in the inaugural parade. They needed 13 12-foot poles to move the flag down the two-mile parade route.
Photograph by David Burnett

A host of military and police units join inaugural planners to form the presidential escort for the parade. Marching elements include the Metropolitan Police, U.S. Capitol Police, U.S. Park Police, U.S. Army Band (Pershing's Own), 3rd U.S. Infantry Fife and Drum Corps (The Old Guard) and ceremonial, honor and color guards of all the military services.
Above: Ken Cedeño

The president, vice president and their wives review the units on the steps of the east front of the Capitol. The military's participation in presidential inaugurations started in 1789, when George Washington was escorted to the steps of Federal Hall in New York City, where he took the first oath of office. *Above: Ken Cedeño*

President and Mrs. Bush and Vice President and Mrs. Cheney enjoy the cheers of parade watchers as they walk the final blocks along Pennsylvania Avenue. More than 200,000 turned out to be a part of this American tradition. Following the official presidential escort, over 11,000 participants marched along the parade route with more than 80 military and civilian marching units, 15 floats and 21 equestrian units. Although many impromptu parades and spontaneous escorts enlivened previous inaugurations, the first officially planned parade was in 1841 after the inauguration of President William Henry Harrison. In 1977, Jimmy Carter and his family were the first to walk the entire parade route from the Capitol to the White House.

Above: Arthur Grace
Left: David Hume Kennerly
Right: Karen Ballard

Grammy, Emmy and Freedom Foundation award-winning director Dr. Craig Jessop conducts the 350 members of the Mormon Tabernacle Choir as their float moves down Pennsylvania Avenue. The Washington Crossing Foundation modeled their float after the famous painting by Emanuel Gottlieb Leutze depicting Washington and his troops crossing the Delaware River on Christmas night, 1776. The crossing, a turning point in the Revolutionary War, is one of the most famous images of our nation's first president.
Above: Anne Day
Left: David Burnett

The Troopers Drum and Bugle Corps from Casper, Wyoming, boasts one of the proudest and richest histories in all of the drum corps activity. Their uniforms are replicas of those worn by the 11th Ohio Cavalry in the late 1800s. Ever building on a championship tradition and dedication to excellence, the corps has been nicknamed, "America's Corps," a title they hold with honor.
Above: David Burnett

Each of the 62 different organizations, floats, bands and roving acts that participated in the parade get a moment of prime time: passing in front of the reviewing stand where the two Presidents Bush, their wives, families and closest friends watch and wave until the main theme float, "Celebrating America's Spirit Together," capped the parade and passed by the White House. For the first time in American history, a former president joined his son on the presidential reviewing stand.

Above: John Ficara
Left above: Robert McNeely
Left below: David Hume Kennerly

The University of Texas Longhorn Band gives
the traditional "Hook 'em Horns" salute.
Photograph by Arthur Grace

Inaugural planners transform
Union Station, a busy commuter
hub by day, into an elegant and
festive ballroom for inaugural
night. The balls are held at nine
locations around the city and are
attended by thousands from
around the country.
Photograph by Anne Day

The Bushes and the Cheneys, arriving in separate motorcades, make appearances and brief remarks at each ball. Traveling with the Bushes are event co-chairs Mr. and Mrs. Bill DeWitt, Mr. and Mrs. Mercer Reynolds and Executive Director Jeanne Johnson Phillips and her husband David Phillips. New Jersey Governor Christine Todd Whitman, nominated as administrator of the Environmental Protection Agency, greets guests at the New Jersey, New York and Pennsylvania ball.
Above: Robin Bowman
Left: Anne Day
Far left: Sam Kittner

They danced until the cows came home at the Texas-Wyoming Ball, one
of three inaugural balls held at the Washington Convention Center.
Photographs by David Alan Harvey

"But first, we've got some dancing to do," President Bush says, before taking the traditional presidential whirl around the floor with Mrs. Bush, which delights the room.
Photograph by Eric Draper

Dipping, dancing, laughing and relishing the moment ... the dancing went on until the early hours of Sunday morning at the Marriott Wardman Park Hotel Inaugural Ball.
Above: Sam Kittner

The Cheneys greet the crowd before taking their turn on the ballroom floor.
Above: Sam Kittner

NATIONAL PRAYER SERVICE OF THANKSGIVING

Family and friends of the president and vice president, along with Cabinet
nominees, members of Congress, transition staff, inaugural staff and the
general public gather at the National Cathedral for an hour long prayer
service that includes choirs, readings and prayer. After the service, President
Bush thanks Rev. Suzanne Harris of St. John's Episcopal Church in Jackson,
Wyoming. The first lady's mother, Mrs. Jenna Welch, and her escort depart
at the conclusion of the service.
Above: David Burnett
Right above and below: David Hume Kennerly
Previous pages: Robert McNeely

On their first full day of the new administration, the Bushes welcome visitors to the White House. More than 4,000 people are greeted and many have an opportunity to see and shake hands with the new chief executive and his wife.
Above: David Burnett
Left: Paul Morse

First dogs Barney and Spot explore
their new front lawn.
Photograph by Paul Morse

Preparing the Oval Office   PHOTOGRAPHS BY DICK SWANSON

A new coat of paint is applied. New drapes are hung. A new carpet is unrolled. The Oval Office is made ready for its new occupant.

A most remarkable moment in American history. Not only is it the first time in 40 years that a father has survived to see his son become president, it's only the second time that a father has been followed into the country's highest office by his son.
Photograph by Eric Draper

The vice president welcomes a large group of supporters and staff to a reception at his new home at the Naval Observatory. With his granddaughter Elizabeth, Dick Cheney spends a private moment.
Photographs by David Hume Kennerly

And so to work. President and Mrs. Bush welcome the new White House Staff who take the oath of office and pledge to uphold the highest standard of conduct to help preserve the honor and dignity of the Office of the President.
Photographs by David Hume Kennerly

President Bush looks out over the south
lawn of the White House as the sun shines
on a new presidency.
Photograph by Eric Draper

MESSAGE FROM THE CO-CHAIRS

MERCER AND GABRIELLE REYNOLDS
KATHY AND BILL DEWITT

Those of us who have been privileged to be involved with the inauguration of the 43rd president of the United States have sought to bring the ceremony and festivities to as many Americans as possible and reach out to all through "Celebrating America's Spirit Together."

Together we are witnessing the orderly transfer of power in the grand and glorious tradition that began on April 30, 1789, when George Washington first took the solemn oath of office as president.

This inaugural is a time for a renewal of the American spirit and a time to look forward with hope to the promise and challenge of the future.

On behalf of the many people involved in the inauguration of George W. Bush and Richard B. Cheney, we wish to join in the spirit of the new administration in reaching out to all Americans to reflect their hopes and dreams in forging the events for the new century.

We believe this is an opportunity to showcase the great heritage of our nation and to make the events surrounding the swearing-in of our new president and vice president a time for all Americans to join together and participate in our nation's grandest and oldest celebration. We are celebrating the diversity of all our people and our shared devotion to the American spirit.

On our behalf we wish to thank all, particularly the many volunteers, who tirelessly worked to make this inauguration a success, and we humbly express our appreciation for having the honor of representing the 54th Presidential Inaugural Committee for our new president in this new century in the true American spirit.

IN GRATEFUL APPRECIATION

FRED MEYER
Chairman
Executive Committee

BRAD FREEMAN
Chairman
Finance

President George W. Bush and Vice President Richard B. Cheney wanted to host a uniquely American celebration - bringing as many Americans together as possible to honor America's unique heritage and to set an optimistic tone for the future. It simply could not have been done without the efforts of thousands of people - military, civilian, as well as committed individuals and companies that provided substantial support to assure that the events reflected the solemnity and the spirit of this new administration.

Their financial and moral support meant that we could orchestrate in less than 31 days, a three-day event that touched and brought together millions of people across the globe. We are proud of the efforts that were made to provide detailed information on the Web and to assure that disabled Americans were able to participate fully. We are also exceptionally pleased that despite the short timetable, everything was completed on schedule and under budget.

We are proud of this legacy and could not have done it without the help of our underwriters and friends. We are deeply grateful for their commitment to the beginning of this new and vibrant administration.

THE 54TH PRESIDENTIAL INAUGURAL COMMITTEE

Co-Chairmen
Kathy and Bill DeWitt
Gabrielle and Mercer Reynolds

Chairman, Executive Committee
Fred Meyer

Finance Chairman
Brad Freeman

Finance Co-Chairmen
Julie Finley
Al Hoffman, Jr.

Executive Director
Jeanne Johnson Phillips

Executive Committee
Mr. and Mrs. Al Austin
Mr. and Mrs. Louis A. Beecherl, Jr.
The Honorable Griffin Bell
Mr. and Mrs. Stuart Bernstein
Mr. and Mrs. Jim Blosser
Mr. and Mrs. Stephen Brauer
Ms. Nancy G. Brinker
Mr. Bill Brisben
Mr. Roger Campos
Mr. Pete Carpenter

Mr. Craig Cason
Mr. and Mrs. Bob Castellini
Mr. and Mrs. Bill Ceverha
Mr. and Mrs. James H. Click
Mr. and Mrs. Chuck Cobb
Mr. Leonard Coleman
Mr. and Mrs. Glenn Collins
Mr. and Mrs. Richard T. Farmer
The Honorable Max Fisher
The Honorable and Mrs. Matt Fong
Mr. and Mrs. Sam Fox
Mr. and Mrs. James B. Francis, Jr.
Mr. and Mrs. David F. Girard-diCarlo
Mr. and Mrs. Tom Grady
Mr. and Mrs. Mark Guzzetta
Mr. and Mrs. Bruce Harrison
Mr. and Mrs. John M. Hennessy
Mr. and Mrs. John F. Hotchkis
Mr. B. Wayne Hughes
Mr. Gaylord T. Hughey, Jr.
Mr. Ray L. Hunt
Mr. and Mrs. Alphonso Jackson
The Honorable and Mrs. Eric M. Javits
Mr. and Mrs. Robert Wood Johnson, IV
Mr. and Mrs. Sheldon B. Kamins
Mr. and Mrs. James C. Kenny
Mr. and Mrs. Richard Kinder
Mr. and Mrs. C. Michael Kojaian

Mr. and Mrs. Floyd Kvamme
Mr. and Mrs. James Langdon, Jr.
Mr. and Mrs. Howard Leach
Mr. and Mrs. Al Lerner
The Honorable and Mrs. Tom Loeffler
The Honorable and Mrs. Bob Martinez
Ms. Bonnie McElveen-Hunter
Mr. and Mrs. Bob Meyerson
Mr. Patrick Michaels, Jr.
Mr. and Mrs. Jim Nicholson
Mr. Jim Oberwetter
Mr. Jack Oliver
Mr. and Mrs. Tony Parker
Mr. and Mrs. Don Powell
Mr. David Pratt
Mr. and Mrs. Heinz Prechter
Mr. James M. Reynolds
Mr. and Mrs. Dub Riter, Jr.
Mr. Raul R. Romero
Mr. and Mrs. Dwight Schar
The Honorable Rockwell A. Schnabel
Mr. Horst Schulze
Ms. Dorrie Scott Eades
The Honorable and Mrs. Mel Sembler
Mr. and Mrs. Allen Shivers
Mr. and Mrs. Clifford Sobel
Mr. and Mrs. Enrique Sosa
Mr. Ronald P. Spogli

Mr. and Mrs. Craig Stapleton
Mr. and Mrs. Warren Stephens
Mr. and Mrs. Peter Terpeluk, Jr.
Mr. Tim Timken
Mr. and Mrs. Ron Weiser
Mr. and Mrs. Ted Welch
Mr. and Mrs. Les Wexner
Mr. George M. Williams
Mr. and Mrs. Roger J. Williams
Mr. Virgil R. Williams
Mr. Selim Zilkha and Mrs. Mary Hayley

Honorary Event Chairpersons

Inaugural Opening Celebration
Joyce and Dick Farmer
Nancy and Ray Hunt
Anne and Ron Walker
Diane and Anthony Williams

Candlelight Dinners
Washington Hilton
Marcia and Alphonso Jackson
Norma and Al Lerner
Edith and Carl Lindner
Maggie and Dick Scarlett
Debbie and Craig Stapleton
Mary and Robert Whilden

THE 54TH PRESIDENTIAL INAUGURAL COMMITTEE

The National Building Museum
Sandy and Jim Langdon
Mary and Joe Meyer
Suzanne and Jim Nicholson
Raul Romero

Union Station
Margaret and Jim Kenny
Kathy and Jamie Reynolds
Janet and Bill Rogers
Betty and Mel Sembler

Laura Bush Celebrates America's Authors
Barbara Bush
Jenna Welch
Nancy Brinker
Jan Bullock
Susie Evans
Debbie Francis
Regan Gammon
Nancy Kinder
Nelda Laney
Jan O'Neill

Inaugural Balls

Ronald Reagan Building
Alice Cary and Lee Brown
Vicki and Jim Click
Susan and Russ Freeman
Natalie and Jim Haslam
Jean and Floyd Kvamme
Gretchen and Howard Leach
Bonnie and Bynum Hunter
Dianne and Bill Moss
Marcia and John Price
Margaret and John Robson
Patty and Jim Simmons
Faye and Alex Spanos

Union Station
Carmen and Jim Courter
Judy and Lew Eisenberg
Connie and David Girard-diCarlo
Margarita and Jack Hennessy
Barbara and Cliff Sobel

D.C. Armory
Stuart and Wilma Bernstein
Patty and Bucky Bush
Lindsey and Scott Bush
Alma and Joe Gildenhorn
Lois and Dick Hug
Lynne and Shelly Kamins
Margaret and Terry O'Donnell
Greg and Bob Royall
Martha and Dwight Schar
Diane and Peter Terpeluk
Maryann and Dirk Van Dongen
Diane and Anthony Williams

Washington Convention Center
Julie and Louis Beecherl
Shirley and John Berry
Bill Brisben
Susie and Bob Castellini
Kathleen and Glenn Collins
Debbie and Jim Francis
Lori and Dave Gribbin
Nancy and Rich Kinder
Norma and Al Lerner
Nancy and Tom Loeffler
Lucinda and Tom Marinis
Jan and Joe O'Neill
Jane and Rob Portman
Twanna and Don Powell
B. J. and Dub Riter
Betty and Mel Sembler
Robin and Bud Shivers
Abigail and Les Wexner
Patty and Roger Williams

National Building Museum (Pension Building)
Columba and Jeb Bush
Betty and Mel Sembler

Washington Hilton
Joy and Boysie Bollinger

Sue Ellen and Joe Canizaro
Taylor and Donald Ensenat
Adele and Don Hall
Wally and Heinz Prechter
Joan and Peter Secchia

Marriott Wardman Park Hotel
Kimmy and Stephen Brauer
Helvetia Barros and Cesar Cabrera
Helen and Fred Cooper
Norma and Jim Edenfield
Michele and Tom Foley
Marilyn and Sam Fox
Karen and Fred Jones Hall
Buck Harless
Kathy and Al Hubbard
Tine and John Palmer
David Pratt
Sheri and Horst Schultze
Caroline and Charles Swindells
Sari and John Turner
Kathy and Ken Zangara

54th Presidential Inaugural Honorary Committee
Mr. Richard T. Aab
Mr. and Mrs. Duane W. Acklie
Mr. Phil Adams
Mr. David G. Albert
Mr. Anthony Alexander
Mr. Joe B. Allen
Mr. W.W. Allen
The Honorable Lincoln Almond
Mr. Paul Anderson
The Honorable Hushang Ansary
Mr. George L. Argyros
Mr. Jorge Arrizurieta
Mr. Alex Arshinkoff
Mr. Robert B. Asher
Mr. Alfred S. Austin
Mr. Bob Babbage
The Honorable James A. Baker, III
Mr. Haley Barbour
Mr. H. Douglas Barclay
Mr. James L. Barksdale
Mr. Sam Barshop
The Honorable Joe Barton
Mr. Lee M. Bass
Mr. Lawrence E. Bathgate
Mr. Bill Batoff
Mr. George S. Bayoud, Jr.
Mr. Henry C. Beck, III
Mr. Louis A. Beecherl, Jr.
Mr. J. Carter Beese
Mr. Craig L. Berkman
Mr. Dennis R. Berman
Mrs. Lea Berman
Mr. Stuart Bernstein
Mr. Tom Bernstein
Mr. Roland W. Betts
The Honorable Teel Bivins
Mr. Rick Blankenship
Mr. Jim Blosser
Mr. Herbert F. Boeckmann, II
Mr. Joseph Bogosian
Mr. Donald T. Bollinger
Mr. Michael M. Boone
Mr. Otis Booth, Jr
The Honorable Rudy Boschwitz
Mrs. Katherine E. Boyd
Ms. Darlene Bramon
Mr. Daniel H. Branch
Mrs. Kimmy Brauer
Mr. Stephen F. Brauer
Mr. Donald L. Bren
Mr. Tim Bridgewater
Ms. Nancy G. Brinker
Mr. Bill Brisben
Mr. Les Brorsen
Mr. C. David Brown, II
Mr. W. L. Lyons Brown, Jr.
Mr. John Browning
Mr. Steven Burd
Mr. Christopher Burnham
Mr. Robert N. Burt
Mr. Fred Bush
The Honorable Jeb Bush
Mr. Jonathan Bush

Mr. Marvin Bush
Mr. Prescott Bush
Mr. William H.T. Bush
Mr. William J. Cabaniss
Mr. Cesar B. Cabrera
Mr. Joseph C. Canizaro
Mr. Stephen Canton
Mr. A.R. "Pete" Carpenter
Mr. Ned Carpenter
Mr. Claiborne Carrington
Mr. Donald J. Carty
Mr. Charles M. Cawley
Mr. William Cellini
The Honorable Paul Cellucci
Mrs. Mary Ceverha
Mr. Paul Ceverha
Mr. John T. Chambers
The Honorable Elaine C. Chao
Mr. Anthony R. Chase
Mrs. Martha Chayet
Mr. Howard Chong
The Honorable and Mrs. William P. Clements
Mr. James H. Click
Mr. Armando Codina
Mr. Leonard Coleman
Mr. Glenn Collins
Mr. Herb Collins
Mr. John Collins
Mr. Peter R. Coneway
Mr. Ross Connelly
Mr. James M. Connolly
Mr. Lodwrick Cook
Mr. Frederick E. Cooper
Mr. Robert P. Corker, Jr.
Mr. Bob Crandall
Mr. Jim Culbertson
The Honorable Alfonse D'Amato
Mr. William J. Danhoff
Mr. John Danilovich
Mr. Robert A. Day
Mr. Robert H. Dedman, Jr.
Mr. Michael S. Dell
Mr. Kenneth T. Derr
Mr. Robert Devlin
Mr. William O. DeWitt
The Honorable Donald T. Di Francesco
Mr. Cortlandt S. Dietler
Mr. Tom Dorr
Mr. John Dowd
The Honorable H.B. Downer, Jr.
The Honorable Jennifer Dunn
Mr. Buzz DuPont
Mr. Patrick Durkin
Mr. Edward W. Easton
Mr. Jim Edenfield
Mr. Richard Egan
Mr. Tom Engibous
The Honorable John Engler
Mr. Roger A. Enrico
The Honorable Donald B. Ensenat
Mr. Melvyn J. Estrin
The Honorable Donald L. Evans
Mr. Tre Evers
Mr. Nelson Fairbanks
The Honorable Lauch Faircloth
Ms. Martha Fallgatter
Mr. Jose Fanjul
Mr. William S. Farish, Jr.
Mr. Richard T. Farmer
Mr. Robert E. Fee
Mr. Thomas M. Ferguson
Mrs. Julie Finley
Mr. Martin Fiorentino
Mr. David Fisher
Mr. Donald G. Fisher
The Honorable Max Fisher
Mr. David Flaum
Dr. C. Edward Floyd
The Honorable Thomas C. Foley
Mr. William P. Foley, II
The Honorable Matt Fong
Mr. Charles T. Foscue
The Honorable M.J. Foster, Jr.
Mr. and Mrs. Jose Fourquet
Mr. Sam Fox
Mr. James B. Francis, Jr.
The Honorable Barbara Hackman Franklin
Mr. Brad Freeman

Mr. Russell Freeman
Mr. Jeff Fuqua
Mr. Bruce S. Gelb
The Honorable Jim Geringer
Mr. Yousif B. Ghafari
The Honorable Joseph B. Gildenhorn
Mr. George Gilmore
The Honorable James Gilmore
Mr. Samuel L. Ginn
Mr. Anthony H. Gioia
Mr. David F. Girard-diCarlo
Mr. Howard Gittis
Mr. Charles L. Glazer
Mr. Al Glickman
Mr. D. Stephen Goddard, Jr.
H.P. Goldfield
The Honorable Stephen Goldsmith
The Honorable Roy M. Goodman
Mr. William H. Goodwin, Jr.
Mr. Bill Gormley
Mr. Robert T. Grand
The Honorable Bill Graves
Mr. Pete Green
Mr. Hank Greenberg
The Honorable Kenny Guinn
Mr. Mark Guzzetta
Mr. Art Hackney
Mrs. Adele Hall
Mr. Frederick J. Hall
Mr. Jon D. Hammes
Mr. Tim Hammonds
Mr. Mark Hanley
Mr. David Hanna
Mr. Jon Hanson
Mr. Buck Harless
The Honorable John Harp
Ms. Pat Harrison
Mr. James A. Haslam, II
Mrs. Rita Hauser
Mr. Joyce Haver
Mr. Richard Heath
Mr. David V. Hedley
Mr. John M. Hennessy
Mr. Robert Herbold
Mr. Hans H. Hertell
Mr. Jim Hewgley
Mr. R. Steven Hicks
Mr. Thomas O. Hicks
Mr. Michael R. Hightower
Mr. and Mrs. Henry L. Hillman
Mr. J. Roger Hirl
Mr. Franklin Hobbs
The Honorable John Hoeven
Mr. Al Hoffman, Jr.
Mr. Robert B. Holland, III
Mr. David Horowitz
Mr. Dudley Horton
Mr. and Mrs. Al Hubbard
Mr. R. D. Hubbard
The Honorable Mike Huckabee
Mr. James Huffines
Mr. Richard E. Hug
Mr. Gaylord T. Hughey, Jr.
Mr. J.C. Huizenga
The Honorable Jane Dee Hull
Ms. Caroline Rose Hunt
Mr. Gary H. Hunt
Mr. Ray L. Hunt
Mr. Jon M. Huntsman, Jr.
Mr. Alphonso Jackson
Mr. Bernie Jackvony
The Honorable William Janklow
The Honorable Eric Javits
Mr. Christopher T. Jenny
The Honorable Mike Johanns
Ms. Brenda Johnson
The Honorable Gary Johnson
Mr. John W. Johnson
Ms. Karen Johnson
Mr. Robert Wood Johnson, IV
Mr. Thomas L. Johnson
Mr. Walter E. Johnson
Ms. Jeanne Johnson Phillips
Mr. Don D. Jordan
Mr. Sheldon B. Kamins
Mr. Stephen Kass
Mr. Ronald C. Kaufman
Dr. Munr Kazmir

The Honorable Francis A. Keating
Mr. Craig Keeland
Mr. Herbert D. Kelleher
The Honorable Dirk Kempthorne
Mr. Ken Kendrick, Jr
Mr. and Mrs. James C. Kenny
Ms. Bobbie Kilberg
Mr. Bill Kilberg
Mrs. Nancy Kinder
Mr. Rich Kinder
Mr. Jim Kittle
Mr. Robert Kjellander
Mr. Jim Klauser
Mr. Charles F. Knight
Mr. Tru Knowles
Mr. David Knowlton
Mrs. Doro Koch
Mr. C. Michael Kojaian
Mr. Donald M. Koll
Mr. Hersh Kozlov
Mr. Thomas R. Kuhn
Mr. Floyd Kvamme
The Honorable Paul C. Lambert
Mr. Raymond J. Lane
Mr. David M. Laney
Mr. Mark Langdale
Mr. and Mrs. James Langdon, Jr.
Mr. Frank Lavin
Mr. Kenneth Lay
Mr. Fred W. Lazenby
Mr. Howard Leach
The Honorable Michael Leavitt
Mr. Winnie LeClercq-Jacques
Mr. W. Howard Lester
Mr. R. Steve Letbetter
The Honorable Andrew L. Lewis
Mr. Adam Lindemann
The Honorable Robert L. Livingston
Mrs. Nancy Loeffler
The Honorable Tom Loeffler
Mr. Jorge Luis Lopez
Mr. Jeff B. Love
Mr. Brian Lunde
Mr. Earle Mack
Mr. John B. Mahaffey
Ms. Adair Margo
Mr. Thomas P. Marinis
Mr. Jack Martin
The Honorable Bob Martinez
Mr. William Martini
The Honorable Judy Martz
The Honorable Scott McCallum
Mr. Frederick D. McClure
Mr. Bill McCormick
Ms. Sharon McCutchin
Ms. Bonnie McElveen-Hunter
Mr. Jim McGlothlin
Mr. and Mrs. William A. McKenzie
The Honorable Ed McMahan
Mr. Colin McMillan
Mr. Dean McWilliams
Mr. Bernard Mendik
Mr. J. Frank Mermoud
Mr. David A. Metzner
Mr. Fred Meyer
Mr. Patrick Michaels, Jr.
Mr. Vance C. Miller
Mr. Reese L. Milner, II
The Honorable David Miner
Mr. Stephan Minikes
Ms. Suzie Mitchell
Mr. Phil Montgomery
Ms. Wilhelmina R. Morian
Mr. H. Gary Morse
Mr. Robert Mosbacher, Jr.
Mr. and Mrs. William Moss
Mr. Dennis Muchmore
Mr. David H. Murdock
Mr. R. Madison Murphy
Mr. Palmer Murray
Mr. Ralph J. Nagel
Mr. Charles D. Nash, Jr.
Mr. Thomas J. Neff
Mr. Patrick M. Nesbitt
Mr. Andres Nevarez
Ms. Bonnie Newman
Mr. Jim Nicholson
Mr. Dennis E. Nixon

The Honorable Anne Northup
Mr. Alan P. Novak
Mr. Erle Nye
Mr. Robert O'Connell
Mr. Joseph J. O'Donnell
Mr. Peter O'Donnell, Jr.
Mr. Brad O'Leary
Mr. Joe O'Neill
Mr. Jim Oberwetter
Mr. Jack Oliver
Mr. John Ong
The Honorable Bill Owens
Mr. Patrick C. Oxford
Mr. William Palatucci
Mr. John N. Palmer
Mr. Steve Papermaster
Mr. Anthony Parker
Ms. Margaret Parker
Mr. Gerald L. Parsky
The Honorable George Pataki
Ms. Barbara S. Patton
Mr. Jim Paul, Jr.
The Honorable L. William Paxon
Mr. Marshall B. Payne
Mr. Stephen P. Payne
Mr. A. Jerrold Perenchio
Mr. Douglas Perry
The Honorable Rick Perry
Mr. Wayne Perry
Ms. Carroll Petrie
The Honorable and Mrs. Joseph Carltom Petrone
Mr. Thomas F. Petway III
Mr. Earl N. Phillips, Jr.
Mr. R. H. Pickens
Mr. Sergio Pino
Mr. Marvin Alvin Pomerantz
Mr. Tom Potter
Mr. Don Powell
Mr. Heinz Prechter
Mr. John Price
Mr. Jerry Prostrollo
Mr. Chesley Pruet
Mr. John S. Rainey
Dr. Ralph Reed
Mr. Warren Reuther
Mr. James M. Reynolds
Mr. Mercer Reynolds
Mr. and Mrs. Walter Rich
The Honorable Tom Ridge
Mr. Dub Riter, Jr.
Mr. Duane R. Roberts
Mr. George Roberts
Mr. Joe Rogers
Mr. Sig Rogich
Mr. Raul R. Romero
Mr. John D. Rood
Mr. Edward W. Rose, III
Mr. Evans Rose
The Honorable John Rowland
Mr. Robert B. Rowling
Mr. Robert V. Royall
The Honorable William Ruckleshaus
Mr. Larry Ruvo
The Honorable George Ryan
Mr. Patrick G. Ryan
Mr. John Saltsman, Jr.
Mr. A. R. Sanchez, Jr.
Mr. David Saperstein
Mr. Dwight Schar
Mr. William Scherer
The Honorable Rockwell A. Schnabel
Mr. Charles Schwab
Mr. Peter F. Secchia
Mr. Taylor Segue
The Honorable Mel Sembler
Mr. Terry Semel
Mr. Nick Serafy
Mr. Donald B. Shackelford
Mr. C. Russell Shearer
Mr. Allen Shivers
Mr. Ned Siegel
Mr. Martin Silverstein
Mr. Jim Simmons
Mr. Sam Simon
The Honorable Samuel K. Skinner
Mr. Gregory W. Slayton
Mr. James Smith
Mr. Clifford Sobel

Mr. William T. Solomon
Mr. Enrique Sosa
Mr. Frank Sourbeer
Mr. Alex G. Spanos
Mr. and Mrs. Paul W. Speltz
Mr. Jerry Speyer
Mr. Ronald P. Spogli
Mr. Manuel N. Stamatakis
Mr. Craig Stapleton
Ms. Debbie Stapleton
Mr. Roger T. Staubach
The Honorable Glenn Steil
Mr. Thomas F. Stephenson
Ms. Jocelyn L. Straus
Dr. Kirk Sullivan
The Honorable Don Sundquist
Mr. Charles J. Swindells
The Honorable Robert Taft
Mr. Peter Terpeluk, Jr.
The Honorable James R. Thompson
Ms. Christine Toretti
Mr. Tony Trimble
Mr. Hank True
Mr. Sol Trujillo
Ms. Donna Tuttle
Mr. Robert Tuttle
The Honorable Cecil Underwood
Mr. Don Upson
Mr. Skip Vallee
Mr. William J. Van Devender
Mr. Dirk Van Dongen
Ms. Rene Vasquez
Mr. Raj Vattikuti
Mr. Jack C. Vaughn, Jr.
Mr. and Mrs. Edward O. Vetter
Dr. R. Vijay
Mr. Frank Visco
Mr. Peter Vlachos
Mr. Raymond T. Wagner
Mr. Tom Wagner
Mr. Jim Wallace
Mr. Roger W. Wallace
Mrs. Heather Hill Washburne
Mr. Fred Webber
Mr. Lee C. Weingart
Mr. Jerry Weintraub
Mr. Thomas W. Weisel
Mr. Ron Weiser
Mr. Ted Welch
The Honorable William F. Weld
Mr. Paul Welday
Ms. Jimmy Westcott
Mr. Les Wexner
Mr. Robert H. Whilden, Jr.
Mr. Dave H. Williams
Mr. George M. Williams
Mr. Roger Williams
Mr. Virgil R. Williams
The Honorable Stephen R. Windom
Mr. Bob Wright
Mr. Charles J. Wyly, Jr.
Mr. Barry Wynn
Mr. Sam Yingling
Mr. Rodger Young
Mr. William Young
Dr. Zach Zachariah
Mr. Kenneth B. Zangara
Mr. Fred S. Zeidman

Underwriters
Abbott Laboratories
Dr. Miriam and Sheldon G. Adelson, Venetian Resort
AEGON
Agua Caliente Band of Cahuilla Indians
Dr. David Alameel
Alcoa
American Airlines
American Council of Life Insurers
American Express
American Financial Group
American Insurance Association
American International Group, Inc.
American Trucking Associations
Judy and John M. Angelo
Anheuser-Busch Companies
The Honorable and Mrs. Hushang Ansary
AOL Time Warner

Archer Daniels Midland Company
Mr. and Mrs. George A. Argyros
AT&T
Robert G. Barrett
Mr. and Mrs. Lee M. Bass
Lawrence E. Bathgate, II
Grace and Tom Benson
Claudia Hawthorne and Dennis Berman
Mr. and Mrs. Tom A. Bernstein and Mr. and Mrs. Roland W. Betts
John and Shirley Berry
Mrs. Marilynn M. Berry
Bessemer Securities Corporation / The Bessemer Group, Inc.
Blank Rome Comisky & McCauley LLP
Blue Cross and Blue Shield of Florida, Inc.
The Boeing Company
BP
Mr. and Mrs. Stephen F. Brauer
Brisben Development, Inc.
Bristol-Myers Squibb Company
Mr. and Mrs. John J. Cafaro
Mr. and Mrs. Joseph C. Canizaro
Linda and Don Carter
Barbara and Finn Caspersen
The Cassidy Companies
Charles M. Cawley, Chairman and CEO, MBNA America Bank
Vicki and Tom Celani
The Chevron Companies
Cisco Systems
Citigroup
Mrs. James H. Clement, Sr.
Mr. and Mrs. Jim Click, Jr.
CMC Company
CMS Energy
The Coca-Cola Company
Mr. Ken W. Cole, Honeywell
Glenn Collins, NeoDyme Technologies Corp.
Frederick E. Cooper
Credit Suisse First Boston
Mr. and Mrs. Robert A. Day
DCS, Inc.
Lawrence J. De George
Dr. A.K. Desai & Jim Holton
Mr. and Mrs. William O. DeWitt, Jr.
James K. Dobbs, III
DOMINION
John F. Donahue
The Dow Chemical Company
Archie W. Dunham, Chairman, President and CEO, Conoco Inc.
EDS
Richard J. Egan
Mr. and Mrs. Lewis M. Eisenberg
Emerson
Irl F. Engelhardt, Chairman and CEO, Peabody Group
Enron
Exxon Mobil Corporation
Fannie Mae
Mr. and Mrs. Nijad I. Fares
Mr. and Mrs. William S. Farish, Jr.
Joyce and Dick Farmer
Farmer's Insurance Group of Companies
Julie Finley
FirstEnergy Corp.
Mr. and Mrs. William P. Foley, II
Ford Motor Company
Cyndee and Tom Foscue
The Founders Group
Mr. and Mrs. Sam Fox
Bradford M. Freeman
Frito-Lay, Inc.
General Electric
General Motors Corporation
Mr. and Mrs. Bert A. Getz
Global Crossing/ Gary Winnick and Lod Cook
GMAC
Goldman, Sachs & Co.
Great Traditions Land and Development Co.
Mrs. Barbara Grimm
Mr. and Mrs. Mark Guzzetta
Mr. Edward H. Hamm
John Hancock Financial Services, Inc.
James H. Harless
Seeme G. and Malik M. Hasan, M.D.
John W. Henry & Company, Inc.

Hicks, Muse, Tate & Furst Incorporated
Nancy and Gus Hillenbrand
Dawn and Al Hoffman
Julianna Hawn Holt and Peter M. Holt
Joan and John Hotchkis
B. Wayne Hughes
Nancy Ann and Ray L. Hunt
Mr. and Mrs. Charles E. Hurwitz
IBM
International Game Technology
International Paper
Invacare Corporation
Mr. and Mrs. Michael Jaharis
Mr. and Mrs. Charles Johnson
Judy and Dennis Jones
J.P. Morgan Chase & Co.
Lawrence Kadish
Munr Kazmir
James J. Kim
Nancy and Rich Kinder
Kmart Corporation
Kraft Foods, Inc.
Robert D. Kramer
Mr. and Mrs. Kenneth G. Langone
Mr. and Mrs. J. Terrence Lanni
Mr. Ronald Lauder
Linda and Ken Lay
Gretchen and Howard Leach
Thomas C. Leppert, Chairman and CEO, The
    Turner Corporation
Steve Letbetter, Chairman and CEO, Reliant
    Energy
The Limited, Inc.
Carl H. Lindner
The Link Group, LLC
Lockheed Martin
Lockheed Martin IMS
Suzanne and James MacDougald
Mag Instruments, Inc.
Marlene and Fred Malek
Marriott International, Inc.
J. and M. McDowell
Dr. Henry A. McKinnell
Timothy P. McKone, SBC Communications
Elizabeth and Drayton McLane, Jr.
Mr. and Mrs. David Mehl
Merck & Co., Inc
Merrill Lynch and Co., Inc.
Barbara and Fred Meyer
Bob Meyerson
Microsoft Corporation
Mr.and Mrs. John A. Moran
Morgan Stanley Dean Witter & Co.
Mr. H. Gary Morse
Motorola
Mr. Rupert Murdoch, Chairman and CEO,
    News Corporation
David H. Murdock
National Association of Homebuilders
Bobbie and John Nau
Nextel Communications
Northwest Airlines
Erle Nye
Occidental Petroleum Corporation
Office of the Commissioner of Baseball
Donald G. Ogilvie, American Bankers
    Association
Mr. and Mrs. Peter O'Malley
James F. Orr, Chariman, President, and CEO,
    Convergys Corporation
Rocco A. Ortenzio, Chairman and CEO of
    Select Medical Corp.
Outback Steakhouse Political Action Committee
John W. Paxton, Sr.
Mr. and Mrs. John Whitney Payson
PepsiCo, Inc.
Mr. and Mrs. A. Jerrold Perenchio
Thomas F. Petway, III
Fred and Stephanie Pezeshkan, Kraft
    Construction Company
Pharmacia Corporation
Philip Morris Companies Inc.
PhRMA
Patty and Bo Pilgrim, Pilgrim's Pride
PMX Industries, Inc.
Mr. David C. Pratt
Heinz C. Prechter and C. Michael Kojaian
PRIMEDIA Inc.

Marcia and John Price
B.M. "Mack" Rankin, Jr. and
    Freeport-McMoRan
Walter Raquet, Executive Vice President, Knight
    Trading Group, Inc.
Andrew K. Rayburn
RAYTHEON
Mr. and Mrs. Mercer Reynolds
Robert C. Rhein Interests, Inc.
Melinda and Robert Rich
Mr. and Mrs. Duane R. Roberts
James E. Rogers, Cinergy Corp.
Deedie and Rusty Rose
Mr. And Mrs. Henry A. Rosenberg, Jr.
Safeway Inc.
Sallie Mae
Mr. and Mrs. Charles R. Schwab
Ambassador Mel and Betty Sembler, The
    Sembler Company
Therese M. Shaheen
Mr. and Mrs. John M. Shanahan
Stephanie and Ned L. Siegel
Ellen and Matthew Simmons
Jeffrey K. Skilling
Barbara and Clifford Sobel
Southern Company
South Florida Partnership
Mr. and Mrs. Alex G. Spanos
Mr. and Mrs. Dean A. Spanos
Mr. and Mrs. Ronald P. Spogli
R. Allen Stanford
Stephens Group, Inc.
Mr. and Mrs. Thomas F. Stephenson
Susan and John Sykes
Dr. John and Dr. Josephine Templeton
Textron
Sue and Tim Timken
Dennis A. Tito
Christine Toretti
Dr. Thomas and Erma Jean Tracy
Trident Capital, Inc.
Tyson Foods, Inc.
Union Pacific Corporation
U.S. Asia Commerical Development Corporation
UST Inc.
Van Beuren Management, Inc.
Visa U.S.A. Inc.
Bruce M. Waldack
Mr. and Mrs. W. Ray Wallace
Walter Wang
The Washington Post Company
The Washington Redskins
Waste Management, Inc.
Eileen and Ron Weiser / Padma and Raj Vattikuti
Mr. and Mrs. Cortright Wetherill, Jr.
Marylou Whitney and John Hendrickson
Wilkes & McHugh, P.A.
Mr. Charles Wyly
Cheryl and Sam Wyly
Selim K. Zilkha

54th Presidential Inaugural Committee Staff

Executive Office
Jeanne Johnson Phillips, Executive Director
Mary S. Farr, Special Deputy to the Executive
    Director
Susan Galen, Executive Assistant
Angela Jones, Executive Assistant
Nicole Herold, Executive Assistant
Maria Gullo, Executive Assistant
Lynn Lunceford, Executive Assistant

Vice Presidential Operations
Ron Walker, Special Deputy, Office of the Vice
    President-elect
Steve Hart, Deputy Director
Marguerite Sullivan, Deputy Director,
    Operations and Friends and Family
Celeste Colgan, Deputy Director, Friends and
    Family
CeCe Kramer, Deputy Director, Scheduling

Mrs. Bush's Office
Clare Pritchett, Director
Kristi Sherrill, Program Coordinator

Special Services
Beverly Shea, Chief Deputy and Director of
    Special Services
Gretchen Purser, Deputy Director
Jim Wray, Special Deputy

Events and Operations
Brian Montgomery, Chief Deputy and Director,
    Special Events and Operations
Judd Swift, Director, Events and Operations
Gordon C. James, Director, Events
Neal Burnham, Deputy Director, Operations
Patrick Rhode, Deputy Director, Operations
Greg Jenkins, Deputy Director, Events – Press
Ed Cowling, Deputy Director, Events
Kim Palmese, Managing Director, Events
Spence Geissenger, Managing Director, Events
Tobin Harvey, Managing Director, Events
Steve Meyers, Managing Director, Events
Dan McCardell, Managing Director, Budget
Phil Leadroot, Managing Director, Security and
    Credentials
C. James Schaefer, IV, Managing Director,
    Publications
Amy E. Lemen, Deputy Managing Director,
    Publications
Damon Moley, Managing Director, Volunteers
C. Thomas McCully, Managing Director,
    Transportation
David B. Balfour, Deputy Managing Director,
    Transportation

Treasury
Eric Bing, Treasurer and Chief Administrative
    Officer
Margee Dotter, Comptroller
Leslie Cole, Deputy Comptroller
Frank Haas, Director of Administration
Robert Ollison, Director of Marketing
Darlene Riley, Director of Human Resources

General Counsel
Ben Ginsberg, General Counsel
Kenneth P. Jones, Deputy General Counsel
John Kelliher, Deputy General Counsel
Eric Kuwana, Deputy General Counsel

Finance
Mary Kate Johnson, Director
Heather Larrison, Deputy Director
Beth Sturgeon, Deputy Director

Official Proceedings and Scheduling
Bob Goodwin, Special Deputy
John Gibbons, Deputy
Bruce Clark, Deputy

Invitations and Ticketing
Mary Fraser, Director of Invitations and
    Ticketing
Denise Lechtenberger, Deputy Director

Public Liaison
Janet Slaughter Eissenstat, Director
Ken Yale, Deputy Director
Ambassador Donald Ensenat, Deputy Director
    for the Diplomatic Corps
Stephen Payne, Deputy Director for
    Congressional Relations
David Thomas, Deputy Director for Political
    Affairs
Cheryle Adams, Volunteer Center Coordinator
Cynthia Huger, Volunteer Coordinator

Communications
Ed Gillespie, Director
Dirk Vande Beek, Deputy Director
Susan Phalen, Press Secretary
Natalie Rule, Press Secretary

**Joint Congressional Committee on Inaugural
    Ceremonies**
The Honorable Mitch McConnell, Chairman
The Honorable Trent Lott
The Honorable Christopher Dodd
The Honorable J. Dennis Hastert
The Honorable Richard K. Armey
The Honorable Richard A. Gephardt

Armed Forces Inaugural Committee
Major General James T. Jackson, US Army,
    Chairman
Brigadier General Elbert N. Perkins, US Army,
    Deputy Chairman
Captain Dede Gibson, US Navy, Chief of Staff
Thomas L. Groppel, Director of Ceremonies
Lt. Colonel Karl M. Johnson, USAF, Executive
    Officer

General Services Administration Inaugural Staff
Toni Lewis-Hazlewood, Chief Operating Officer
M.A. "Skip" Gerdes, Deputy Chief Operating
    Officer
Lesly Wilson, Counsel
Denise Johnson, Special Assistant and Chief of
    Administration
Patricia Duncan, Chief Procurement Officer
Ralph Boldt, Assistant Chief Operating Officer
    for Security
Sonny Cook, Assistant Chief Operating Officer
    for Operations
Christopher Davis, Chief Funds Control Officer
Saundra Guyton, Chief Telecommunications
    Officer
Willie Mills, Federal Supply Service
Paul Houston, Chief Information Technology
    Officer

Office of Diversity
Ernie Ladd, Special Advisor to the Committee
Eli Rodriguez, Special Advisor to the Committee

**54th Presidential Inaugural Publications
    Division**

With grateful appreciation for all the many
volunteers, staff members and military
professionals whose dedication and countless
hours made this a celebration to long be
remembered.

Standing, left to right: Pim Doerr, Michael R.
Davis, Lauren Hoffer, Barbara Cebuhar, F. C.
Duke Zeller, Jain Lemos, Matthew Naythons,
Heather M. Shockney, Elizabeth Dial, Chris
Paulitz, and Sudhakar N. Kosaraju. *Seated*: C.
James Schaefer, IV, Managing Director, and Amy
E. Lemen, Deputy Director. *Not pictured*:
Suzanne Chase, Charles Lahey, Nancy Long.
*Photograph by Eric Long, Smithsonian
Institutuion*

ABOUT THIS BOOK

The photographs in *Celebrating America's Spirit Together* were created by 20 photojournalists shooting over 1,000 rolls of film during inaugural week. Collectively, these remarkable photographers have captured over 100 presidential inaugurations.

Photographs in this book were made with the most advanced professional film available:

Kodak Professional Supra 400 Film, Kodak Professional Supra 800 Film
Kodak Professional Portra 160NC Film, Kodak Professional Portra 400NC Film
Kodachrome 64 Professional Film/PKR, Kodachrome 200 Professional Film/PKL
Kodak Professional Ektachrome Film E100S, Kodak Professional Ektachrome Film E200
Kodak Ektachrome 320T Professional Film
Kodak T-Max 100 Professional Film/TMX, Kodak T-Max 400 Professional Film/TMY
Kodak T-Max P3200 Professional Film/TMZ

Special thanks to Canon U.S.A., Inc. Professional Markets Department for their help and support, to Central Florida Press, and to the staff at Chrome Photographic of Washington DC: Rob Rowe, David Lingua, Jay Howard, Cris McCarthy, and Gina Kang; and thanks to Binney & Smith, The Mormon Tabernacle Choir, Alex Castro, Col. S. Hoehne, Sandy H. Miller, Tad Prado, Staff Sgt. Annie Proctor, Nancy Ward, and Derek Wilcox.

Contributing Photographers:

Karen Ballard
Robin Bowman
Dennis Brack
David Burnett
Ken Cedeño
Anne Day
Eric Draper
Hector Emanuel
John Ficara
Arthur Grace
Dirck Halstead

David Alan Harvey
Darryl Heikes
David Hume Kennerly
Sam Kittner
John Lamb
Eric Long
Wally McNamee
Robert McNeely
Paul Morse
Dick Swanson

Photograph by Robin Bowman